M000114073

HOPE FOR THE HOLLOW

A Thirty-Day Inside-Out Makeover for Women

Recovering from Eating Disorders

by

Jena Morrow

HOPE FOR THE HOLLOW: A Thirty-Day Inside-Out Makeover for Women
Recovering from Eating Disorders
by Jena Morrow
Published by Lighthouse Publishing of the Carolinas
2333 Barton Oaks Dr., Raleigh, NC, 27614

ISBN 978-1-938499-27-2
Copyright © 2013 by Jena Morrow
Cover design by Ted Williams www.wisdomhousebooks.com
Book design by Reality Info Systems www.realityinfo.com

Available in print from your local bookstore, online, or from the publisher at:
www.lighthousepublishingofthecarolinas.com

For more information on this book and the author visit:
www.jenamorrow.com

All rights reserved. Non-commercial interests may reproduce portions of this
book without the express written permission of Lighthouse Publishing of the
Carolinas, provided the text does not exceed 500 words. When reproducing
text from this book, include the following credit line: "HOPE FOR THE
HOLLOW by Jena Morrow published by Lighthouse Publishing of the
Carolinas. Used by permission."

Library of Congress Cataloging-in-Publication Data
Morrow, Jena.
HOPE FOR THE HOLLOW / Jena Morrow 1st ed.

Printed in the United States of America

Lighthouse Publishing
of the Carolinas
www.lighthousepublishingofthecarolinas.com

Praise for Hope for the Hollow

This book is full of true nourishment for the hungry souls of those suffering with eating disorders. I hope many will receive the life and truth and peace in these words. I'm excited to have it as a resource for my clients.

~ Nancy M. Rivas, Ph.D., Licensed Clinical Psychologist, Meier Clinics & Timberline Knolls

Jena is a sojourner of truth, helping others escape the slavery of an eating disorder. If you need a friend while traveling the recovery path, *Hope for the Hollow* is a wise and joyful companion.

~ Jane Cairo, LCSW, Psychotherapist, Chaplain, co-author of I Can't, God Can, I Think I'll Let Him

Jena Morrow embodies the dramatic transformation that awaits any woman brave enough to choose freedom over fear. In *Hope for the Hollow*, her gentle wisdom inspires readers to hold on to hope, until they, like Jena, become evidence of its promise.

~ Constance Rhodes, Founder, FINDINGbalance; author, Life Inside the Thin Cage

I always have my eye out for new material that helps build upon the whole-person approach to treatment we utilize at The Center, so it is a joy to discover *Hope for the Hollow: A Daily Inside-Out Makeover for Women Recovering from Eating Disorders* Jena Morrow's voice is a friendly, refreshing, inspiring one that not only makes daily change seem possible, but pleasurable. I highly recommend it to women in recovery who are interested in exploring a whole new world of self-care.

~ Gregory Jantz, PhD, founder of The Center for Counseling and Health Resources

Dedication

For the women of Timberline Knolls ...
for your bravery, courage, and strength.
Each and every one of you, past, present, and future,
is an inspiration to me.

Table of Contents

A WORD FROM THE AUTHOR 1

DAY 1: GOTTA START SOMEWHERE 3

DAY 2: WHO AM I? 6

DAY 3: JESUS, TAKE THE WHEEL 9

DAY 4: BOUGHT AND PAID FOR 12

DAY 5: IT'S JUST FOOD! 15

DAY 6: FOR THE FUN OF IT 19

DAY 7: ALL OR NOTHING 22

DAY 8: HONEST TO GOD
Principle #1: Honesty 27

DAY 9: HOPE FOR THE HOLLOW
Principle #2: Hope 30

DAY 10: I SURRENDER ALL...AGAIN
Principle #3: Faith 34

DAY 11: TAKE COURAGE!
Principle #4: Courage 38

DAY 12: WITH ALL MY HEART
Principle #5: Integrity 41

DAY 13: IF YOU ARE WILLING ...
Principle #6: Willingness 45

DAY 14: I CAN'T...GOD CAN...I'LL LET HIM
Principle #7: Humility 49

DAY 15: KEEP ON KEEPIN' ON
Principle #8: Discipline/Perseverance 52

DAY 16: DON'T DRINK THE POISON!
Principle #9: Forgiveness 55

DAY 17: WHY ASK WHY?
Principle #10: Acceptance 59

DAY 18: GROWING PAINS
Recovery Principle #11: Knowledge and Awareness 64

DAY 19: GRATITUDE ADJUSTMENT
Principle #12: Gratitude 67

DAY 20: HELP A SISTER OUT 71

DAY 21: RECOVERY ISN'T THE GOAL 74

DAY 22: NO WORRIES 77

DAY 23: REPROGRAMMING 81

DAY 24: TIMELESS BEAUTY 85

DAY 25: SELF-SABOTAGE 88

DAY 26: THE ONLY WAY OUT IS THROUGH 92

DAY 27: SHHH...REST 95

DAY 28: CAREFUL NOW... 99

DAY 29: BUT FOR THE GRACE OF GOD 102

DAY 30: A NEW SONG 105

WHO AM I IN CHRIST? 108

ACKNOWLEDGEMENTS 113

A WORD FROM THE AUTHOR

When my memoir, *Hollow* (Moody Publishers) was released in 2010, I was overwhelmed by the response it received from readers across the United States, and even as far as Australia and New Zealand. I began receiving numerous Facebook messages and emails from readers. Women continually approached me at book signings and conferences, tearfully telling me how they had been struggling, some with debilitating body dissatisfaction and some with full blown eating disorders, often in complete silence. Still others have called in when they heard me on radio broadcasts, expressing their gratitude to me for telling my story, because it gave them the freedom and courage to share their own—many for the very first time. Nearly all of those with whom I've spoken have expressed a common desperate longing for hope, and their collective need was the inspiration for this book.

In my work at Timberline Knolls Residential Treatment Center, I've had the honor of working with hundreds of courageous women in the fight of their lives as they battled their diseases, daring to speak the unspeakable and face the fears that for years had enslaved them. Some of those brave women have made their way onto these pages and while their names have been changed for confidentiality, their stories of hope are quite real. For all they have shared and taught me, I am truly grateful.

Eating disorders are sinister, tenacious diseases which thrive on secrecy, deception, and shame. Their capacity for destruction is great, but take heart...the healing love and power of the One True God is far greater. He is our hope and His Word is our light. It is my prayer that, as you work through this book, His words will eclipse my own.

As one who has battled anorexia personally, I walk this recovery journey beside you and it is with great joy and gratitude that I profess Jesus Christ is my strength, my comfort, and my deliverer. It is only because of His amazing love and faithfulness I have this hope to share. May His Spirit meet you in these pages, and may He be as near and real to you as He has become to me.

DAY 1: GOTTA START SOMEWHERE

For God is working in you, giving you
the desire to obey him and the power
to do what pleases Him.

Philippians 2:13 NLT

"I don't want to recover," Leah said to me after group, tears standing in her ice-blue eyes. "But I *want* to want it. Does that make any sense?"

I nodded, offering her a gentle smile. It made perfect sense to me. After all, when it comes to recovery from an eating disorder, we gotta start somewhere.

Leah was in a difficult place in her recovery journey— the very beginning. "Pre-contemplation" is the phase of change wherein we have not yet decided what it's worth to us to change and have not yet made a commitment to anything. We're just thinking about recovery, or maybe even just thinking *about* thinking about it. We're turning the idea over in our mind, putting "recovery" on the table and then stepping back a few paces to survey it, walk circles around it, and consider it from all angles. You may find yourself in this very place of pre-contemplation right now and I want you to know that it's perfectly okay to be right where you are.

The fact that you've picked up this book, whether you ordered it or received it from your therapist or a friend who cares for you, means that part of you wants to be well or is at least curious about what it might be like to recover and live life without your eating disorder.

Let's park there for just a minute. What *would* it mean to recover? What risk does it pose? What promises lie behind the door to recovery for you? Recovery itself cannot be the goal. Actually, it is too vague. Recovery isn't the prize; it's the key to prizes yet unknown. What will recovery unlock for you? What will it enable you to dream, to strive for, or to lay hold of?

It may be very new and unfamiliar for you to allow yourself to think this way, in terms of possibility. We will be doing a lot of that in this book, so I challenge you to get used to it.

Below are some reflection questions to help you get started. Remember, where you are is where you are, so I encourage you to let go of any judgment you may have toward yourself for being in this place and to release yourself into "possibility thinking." Ready, set, go!

FOOD FOR THOUGHT

1. Can you relate to Leah when she says she *wants to want recovery*? How so?

2. Scripture isn't just a book; it is God's personal letter to you, His beloved. Do you believe that? If so, personalize today's scripture passage, using your own name in the text. Now read it that way, out loud to yourself.

3. What was it like to read God's promise in that way? Do you believe He is acting in you and will cause you to want to do what pleases Him? Why or why not?

4. How does today's scripture relate to you in your recovery journey?

Father God, You know all things. My ambivalence about recovery is not hidden from You. Thank You for seeing me and meeting me right where I am. As I begin this journey with You in this book, I choose to trust You one day at a time. Thank You for always honoring my decision to trust.

DAY 2: WHO AM I?

You are a chosen people. You are a kingdom of priests, God's holy nation, his very own possession. This is so you can show others the goodness of God, for he called you out of the darkness into his wonderful light. Once you were not a people; now you are the people of God.

1 Peter 2:9-10 NLT

If you have an eating disorder, you are in crisis. Possibly a physical crisis, and certainly an emotional and spiritual one, but the crisis we will deal with today is the one that keeps you a stranger to yourself. Your eating disorder has trapped you in an identity crisis.

Who are you, my friend? I mean, who are you, *really*? What qualities define you in your deepest parts? What makes you, *you*? It has been said that eating disorders have the centripetal force of black holes. They pull and pull, deeper and harder, until they succeed in drawing you away from the things that once gave your life meaning and purpose. When this begins to happen, it is ever so easy to become hard of hearing, missing the voice of our Creator when He whispers to our hearts, "You are mine."

And therein lies your true identity. You are a daughter of the King—a child of God , chosen and set apart for a purpose greater than yourself. He made you and calls you His masterpiece (Ephesians 2:10). You are truly one of a kind. If anyone knows who you are, who you really and truly are, He does. In your search for identity, you may have looked to small gods like comfort, thinness, and perfection to attempt to define yourself, but these are false identities; counterfeits for the real thing.

The real thing is: You—wonderful you. Beautiful, unique, amazing you. The problem at hand is that the eating disorder has blinded you to who *you* really are, and losing the blindfold is a process, a process of learning to see. When our eyes have been hidden in darkness for years and years, it can truly take time to adjust to the light, but as we begin to adjust...as we begin to see our true image and identity...as we begin to see ourselves as reflections of the indescribable beauty of the One True God...we get to know ourselves as who we were created to be.

FOOD FOR THOUGHT

1. What are some of the "small gods" you have looked to for your sense of identity in the past?

2. What are your fears about discovering who you are apart from your disease?

3. How have you allowed your eating disorder to define you throughout the process of your illness?

4. What parts of yourself and your personality do you hope to discover or rediscover as you begin this process of letting go?

(Note: For further study, see "Who am I in Christ?" at the end of the book.)

God, even when I no longer know who I am, I take comfort in knowing that You created me. You laid out the blueprint of my unique design and personality. I thank You for never losing sight of me. I am looking to You to remove my blindfold. I am up for the adventure of rediscovering who I truly am.

DAY 3: JESUS, TAKE THE WHEEL

Then Jesus went to work on his disciples.
Anyone who intends to come with me has to
let me lead. You're not in the driver's seat;
I am. Don't run from suffering; embrace it.
Follow me and I'll show you how. Self-help
is no help at all.

Matthew 16:24-25 MSG

I like to drive. One of my favorite things to do is to get in my car, crank up the music, and hit the open road, with no destination in mind. Driving is fun for me. I enjoy it. And sometimes, I admit, when I am on a trip and another person is driving, I get a little antsy. They might drive too fast or, worse yet, too slow. They might ride the brakes or switch lanes too often or swerve onto the shoulder once in a while. The point is this: I don't like to let people drive if they're not going to drive the way *I* would.

Can you believe the audacity of Jesus, telling those

disciples they had to let Him lead? He tells them they are not in the driver's seat of their lives if they want to follow Him, and then He goes right on to tell them not to run from suffering, which pretty much infers that He is gonna "drive them" head-on right into some suffering at some point on the journey. So why would they let Him lead? And why should we?

Much of our suffering was not in God's Plan A for our lives, but it is simply the natural result of choices we have made. Like any good parent, Father God allows us to reap what we sow, and He allows circumstances to befall us when we have acted in such a way as to invite them into our lives. And, to be fair, suffering isn't always a result of disobedience on our part. Sometimes suffering is just part of the package of living in this fallen world. If we allow it, suffering will lead us right where we need to be—closer to Jesus. Suffering is required for growth.

Our eating disorders have caused us a great deal of suffering: physical pain, discomfort, emotional and spiritual distress, and the pain of seeing how our disease affects others. But letting go of that suffering and letting Jesus take the wheel will not safeguard us from further, different kinds of suffering. Surrendering to the recovery process will not absolve us from suffering, as much as we wish it would. No, suffering will continue to be in our lives, but Jesus promises that as we accept it and trust Him to lead us through, He will never leave us. He will stay at our side and in our heart, and as we let Him navigate, we will grow closer to Him as our steadfast traveling companion.

Jesus will not drive us out of the path of suffering. But since we're going to face suffering anyway, I for one would much rather face it knowing He is in the driver's seat and I never ride alone.

FOOD FOR THOUGHT

1. What do you think the Message translation of our scripture reading means by "self-help is no help at all?" Do you agree?

2. When you are on a road trip with friends or family, do you prefer to drive or to simply come along for the ride? Regardless of your preference, why do you think you prefer it that way?

3. If God is all-powerful and could stop suffering from entering into our lives, why do you suppose He allows it?

4. How has your eating disorder caused suffering in your life? In the lives of those you love?

Father God, I admit that I have struggled with allowing You to occupy the driver's seat in my life. Thank You for always being willing to take the wheel the moment I bring myself to switch seats with You. Just for today, I trust You to drive me safely through my life and my recovery journey.

DAY 4: BOUGHT AND PAID FOR

*Or didn't you realize that your body is a
sacred place, the place of the Holy Spirit?
Don't you see that you can't live however
you please, squandering what God paid such
a high price for? The physical part of you is
not some piece of property belonging to the
spiritual part of you. God owns the whole
works. So let people see God in and through
your body.*

1 Corinthians 6:19-20 MSG

"I think of my body like an old Kleenex—something to be used and then thrown away."

"My body is disgusting. It's proof of how weak and greedy and gluttonous I really am."

"I haven't looked at myself in a mirror in over four years and the only way I can get through the day is to keep reminding myself, 'Just don't look down.' I cope with the shame of my body by just pretending it isn't there."

I hear these sorts of heartbreaking statements from women every day, especially those in the earliest stages of eating disorder treatment. By the time a woman arrives for treatment, she has usually been listening to "old tapes" and lies about her body for a long time, and it becomes essential to begin challenging those lies immediately.

Our scripture passage from 1 Corinthians 6 is specifically referring to the subject of sexual immorality, but God's heart toward us is clearly communicated and easily applied to the abuse we subject our bodies to through disordered eating. In essence, the Spirit of God is saying to us, "Hey—you are mine. I paid dearly for you. Your body is bought and paid for and you belong to Me, not to yourself. I live in your body, so take good care of it for me. And let others see Me reflected in you—not only in your spirit, but in your body too."

Wait...we don't belong to ourselves? How can that be? Isn't my own body the one thing I can rightfully control? So you thought, and many of us think this way: "I can use and abuse my body if I want to. It's not like I'm hurting anyone else. I'm only hurting myself. So it's not a big deal."

Oh, but it's a very big deal to God. Your body is not only His creation, but His acquisition as well. He purchased you for Himself and paid the highest possible price for you. He paid for you with precious, innocent, sinless blood. He wanted you that badly. He made the ultimate sacrifice so that HE might call you—and your body—His own. What are you willing to sacrifice for Him?

FOOD FOR THOUGHT

1. In what ways have you, through your eating disorder, been squandering what God paid such a high price for?

2. What might it mean for others to see God in and through your body?

3. You belong to God and not to yourself. How do you feel about that concept?

4. Do you need to make amends to the Holy Spirit for any ways in which you might have disrespected His sacred place? If so, use your journal to do so. Remember, it's His kindness that leads us to repentance—not because He wants to shame us but because He longs to be close to us.

God, thank You for wanting me enough to purchase me with Your very life. I acknowledge that I do not belong to myself but rather to You. My body is the temple of the Holy Spirit and it is a sacred place. Help me, in gratitude and obedience, to handle my body with care.

DAY 5: IT'S JUST FOOD!

For you are a slave to whatever controls you.

2 Peter 2:19 NLT

I have learned something new from each of the special and unique women I have worked with in residential eating disorder treatment. Together, we worked to discover the tricks that would be helpful to them as they battled their diseases daily. For a young woman named Amy, three little words became especially effective in getting her through meal times early on in her recovery: "It's just food."

Amy had created a pattern, as many of us do, of giving food far more power in her life than it was ever meant to have. For Amy, eating caused her to feel her emotions. If she didn't eat, she was numb, but if she ate, intense emotions came flooding into her heart just as the food came into her system. Food became guilt. Food became shame. Food was loneliness, abandonment, and fear, as well as a flood of unspeakable traumatic memories.

For the first several weeks of treatment, Amy would tremble violently after a meal, overwhelmed by a swell of unidentifiable feelings, until she would force her way into the bathroom to rid herself of both the food and the feelings, emerging numb once again.

Understand this, dear one: Food need not have this kind of power in our lives. God created food for the nourishment of our bodies. He created it and provides it so that we might fuel and strengthen ourselves to carry out the work He gives us, to live life to the full (John 10:10), and to have energy to live out and enjoy our days on earth.

But for women blinded by the powerful lies of an eating disorder, food takes on extraneous significance. It becomes poison, or lover, or constant companion, or threatening abuser. Ultimately, food becomes an object of love or fear...or both. Whether one's life becomes devoted to the terrified avoidance of food or the violent cycle of taking it in and tossing it back, food becomes *master*.

If this is the case for you, think back. Can you recall a "before?" Was there a time in your life when food was just...food? When clothes were just clothes and fitting rooms weren't scary and you actually fed yourself for the purpose of sustaining energy for life? Can you recall a time when food did not have a number value attached to it and your body wasn't a constant source of judgment and shame? Can you remember freedom?

Some of you will remember, and some will not. Some of you will swear you "came this way" with a peculiar tendency to gravitate toward the self-destruct button. But I assure you, beloved, you did not. Brokenness, lies, and wounds have led you here and there is One who stands by, lovingly and longingly, to lead you back out.

Say it with me: "It's just food." It really is. And it always has been.

FOOD FOR THOUGHT

1. People are slaves to whatever has mastered them. Does food seem to have mastered you?

2. How do you know? What sort of red flags might indicate to you that you are currently being mastered by your ED symptoms and behaviors?

3. Ultimately food becomes an object of love or fear...or both. Do you agree? If so, which has food become to you? How so?

4. Recall a time in your life from "before"—a time when you were not mastered by either your love or fear of food. Take time to write out some of the memory of that time in your journal. (If you cannot recall such a time, imagine yourself free of ED's mastery and journal about what that might be like.)

Lord, I know You created food for a very practical reason, but for me to enjoy as well. Your word tells me that I cannot serve two masters. Help me to choose to follow and obey You over the commands and obsessive thoughts of my eating disorder. Help me to remember that it's just food, and whether I love it or fear it, it has no power over me because I belong to You, and through You I am more than a conqueror!

DAY 6: FOR THE FUN OF IT

Such regulations indeed have an appearance of wisdom, with their self-imposed worship, their false humility, and their harsh treatment of the body, but they lack any value in restraining sensual indulgence.

Colossians 2:23 NIV

I remember walking with Kelly, a forty-one-year-old mother in treatment for anorexia, and asking her about her fitness routine at home. "What kind of movement do you most enjoy?"

My heart sank as she answered through a frown. "It isn't about fun for me. It's hours and hours on the machines at the gym, just focusing on the numbers in my head and the pain in my body. That's what exercise is for me."

I found Kelly's statement to be incredibly sad and I hope you do too.

What are we trying to prove to ourselves when we

exercise obsessively for the "harsh treatment of the body?" Do you move your body for the freedom and fun of moving, or to work your body into submission to your unrealistic and tyrannical ideals? Is your body a means of healthy self-expression through dance or sports or play? Or is your body simply an extension of yourself that you have come to treat with little care or respect?

God, in His incredible creativity, designed our bodies for movement. Children are generally thrilled when they discover as toddlers the amazing things their little bodies can do. They run, jump, leap, sway, dance, skip, twirl, and hop at every opportunity. And why? For the fun of it.

When was the last time you moved your body for fun? Exercise doesn't have to be a chore (or worse, a form of self-harm, when taken to unhealthy extremes). God is good and loving and He created our bodies both for productivity and work, as well as for fun and recreation. When Kelly frowned, telling me about the "numbers in her head" as she exercised, she realized the tragedy. She had been missing the point of movement and fitness. She had cheated herself.

What kind of movement is fun for you? Do you like to ride your bike? Climb rocks? Hike the mountains? Jump on a trampoline, play soccer in the backyard, swim, rollerblade, run through the sprinkler? Do it and enjoy yourself. Exercise was *never* intended to be a punishment for eating. We eat to fuel our bodies so that our bodies can be strong. When you move your body today, focus on the wonder of all you can do, and celebrate the strength you are developing as you begin to fuel yourself healthfully.

You can run! You can jump! You can dance! How cool is that?

FOOD FOR THOUGHT

1. Do you identify with Kelly's description of exercise? How so?

2. If you have been exercising "for the harsh treatment of the body," what do you suppose you may have been trying to prove to yourself and/ or others?

3. What are three kinds of movement or activity that you find especially enjoyable? Challenge yourself to be honest about choosing three you most *enjoy*—not the three that necessarily burn the most calories. Don't cheat yourself out of moving for fun.

4. Think of a time in your childhood when you enjoyed moving for the fun of it. Use your journal to descriptively write about that memory.

God, thank You for creating my body to move. Help me to focus on the wonder of all that my body is capable of doing. Teach me to praise You as I enjoy movement and activity for the fun of it. You are so good.

DAY 7: ALL OR NOTHING

How long will you simple ones love your simple ways?

Proverbs 1:22 NIV

Kara pointed disdainfully at the cup of frozen yogurt on her tray, curling her lip back in a disapproving sneer. "I can't have that," she said, leaning away from the table as though her food might bite her.

"Really?" I challenged. "Why can't you have that?"

Kara shook her head, still sneering. "It's a dessert."

I smiled. "It's a dairy."

"It's a dessert," Kara insisted. "It counts as a dairy, but it's still a dessert."

"Kara," I replied, "your body doesn't care whether you call it dessert. It will use the calcium to strengthen your bones and it will use the carbohydrates to give you energy. What does it matter if we call it a dairy or a dessert?"

Tears stood in Kara's round brown eyes. "It's...*sweet*."

"Yes," I agreed. "It's delicious. Tell me again why you can't have it."

"I can't have dessert."

"Because?"

"It's just a rule I have."

Kara wasn't alone. Many women who battle eating disorders devise systems of rules and rituals to impose rigidly upon themselves as a means of creating an illusion of safety and control. For women like Kara, food is militantly categorized: good versus bad, allowable versus forbidden, fear foods versus safe foods. These categories, they believe, safeguard them against losing control. But let's get real. If a cup of frozen yogurt can make a grown woman cry, that control has already changed hands. Sitting in tears at the lunch table, Kara was not in control, but rather she was *controlled*—by her fear—by her rules—by her all-or-nothing thinking.

Little by little, we worked with Kara to challenge the framework of food rules that had become her prison. Over the course of several months, Kara worked with her treatment team and her dietician to identify the false beliefs she had developed about food and eating, and then our job was to help her challenge them with the truth.

If you, too, are enslaved by a system of false beliefs and all-or-nothing thinking, it will be helpful to do what Kara did. Make a list of your false beliefs as they arise (usually at mealtimes or just after), and leave a space to answer them back with God's Truth as He gives it to you.

**Example:

- False belief: Carbs are bad for me and will make me fat. I can't eat bread, pasta, or potatoes. Truth: Carbs are the best source of fuel for my body and I need a regular supply. I can maintain a healthy weight even when I eat some high-carb foods in moderation.

- False belief: I can't eat any fat. It is gross and will make me fat. You are what you eat. Truth: Fats are nutrients, included in God's design for healthy eating.

- False belief: I can't eat this dessert. It will make me gain weight. Truth: That's impossible. One serving of anything cannot do that to me. It takes a lot of extra eating, usually days, to gain *just one pound* of body tissue.

- False belief: I can't have dinner tonight because I've gained two pounds since this morning and I haven't even eaten that much. Truth: I'm measuring fluid shifts. It's normal for the body to retain fluid later in the day.

- False belief: I can't eat anything unless I know exactly how many calories and fat grams are in it. And I need to personally measure out the right portions. Truth:

This practice is intensifying my food fears and an obsessive mindset. God didn't intend for eating to be so complicated.

It may seem awkward and silly at first to talk back to yourself like this, but it's important that we learn to talk back to our disease rather than just letting it continue to feed us lies that go unchallenged. Besides, we all *talk* to ourselves; our problem is that we haven't learned how to *interrupt* ourselves.

ED's "rules" do not have to rule us, and there is a way out of the web of obsession and rigidity. So, how long will you continue to be trapped in your simple ways of black-and-white rules and all-or-nothing thinking?

FOOD FOR THOUGHT

1. Do you identify with Kara's strict adherence to her food rules? What sort of rules have/had you placed upon yourself and your eating?

2. Can you identify with any of the false beliefs given as examples? Which ones?

3. Why do you suppose it is important that we learn to interrupt ourselves?

4. Use your journal to list some of your rules and/ or false beliefs about food, eating, your body, etc. Be sure to think of other areas such as rules around rest and exercise. Leave space after each one so you can return later and answer back with

truth as God reveals it to you. Some of it He may already have revealed to you through your therapist, dietician, etc. Feel free to write those in.

Father God, I know that Your desire is for me to live free of my self-imposed rules and rigidity. Thank You for purchasing my freedom. Teach me to walk freely in it as I trust You. I declare that I no longer live by my rigid all-or-nothing thinking. I have been given the mind of Christ and I have not been given a spirit of fear but of love, power, and a sound mind.

**False Belief and Truth statements used by permission: Ann Capper, RD, CDN: *Food Is Not Alive: Changing the Tapes in Our Heads* (Hungry for Hope conference, 2010).

DAY 8: HONEST TO GOD
Principle #1: Honesty

Would not God have discovered it, since He knows the secrets of the heart?

Psalm 44:21 NIV

Today we begin moving into the spiritual principles behind the Twelve Steps, and it is fitting that we begin with an exploration of the principle of honesty. The further we progress into self-exploration, the more important it becomes to be purposeful about not only getting honest, but staying honest—with others, with ourselves, and with God.

It's been said that a half-truth is a whole lie and sometimes as we move deeper into our recovery work, we can become torn, wanting to please our treatment team, our therapist, our friends and family—and still wanting (desperately at times) to hang on to and "please" our eating disorders. And so we play both sides, sometimes even unconsciously. A friend may ask if we'd like to have lunch, and perhaps we answer that we've already eaten, omitting the detail that what we ate was, say, an apple (hardly a meal). Or maybe your doctor asks if you've been purging and you answer "no," based upon the fact that you haven't yet purged *today*.

Half-truths, as far as God is concerned, are indeed whole lies. And what's more, it doesn't quite matter who we are able to fool with our cleverly disguised lies of omission, because God Himself is the head of our treatment team, and there is no fooling God. He sees all. He knows all. Nothing gets past Him, not even those things we do not dare to admit to ourselves.

But here's the good news: None of it taints or even touches His amazing love for us. God looks at our hearts—clearly, precisely, penetratingly. The contents of our heart are laid bare before Him, because He is the God who sees. He is light and there is no darkness in Him, so He sees all, all the time. All is all He can see.

The difference between being honest with others and being honest with God is that the knowledge of others often depends upon our choice to reveal the truth, but God's knowledge is entirely unaffected by, and independent from, our disclosure. He knows it all anyway. He loves us anyway. And when we truly grasp this, it frees us up to begin moving toward God in truth and transparency, thus tearing the veil that feels as if it separates us from Him, keeping us from intimate prayer and relationship with Him.

Honesty with God is an invitation to be truly known.

FOOD FOR THOUGHT

1. With whom do you find it most challenging to be completely honest—yourself, others, or God? Why?

2. How does it feel to know that God knows absolutely everything you do, say, and think at all times?

3. Which areas of your life are you most likely to lie about? How are you most tempted to lie—by omission, when asked a direct question, when under pressure, etc?

4. Is there ever a time, in the context of recovery, when it is okay to tell a half-truth? Why or why not?

5. Write out a prayer in your journal, confessing to God any lies you have told that you have gotten away with recently. As you do so, remember what awaits you: forgiveness, love, and a fresh start.

Father God, I confess that my eating disorder has caused me to be dishonest with myself, with others, and with You. With Your help, I am willing to change, and I ask You to empower me to live and walk in transparency and truth. Thank You for loving me, no matter what.

DAY 9: HOPE FOR THE HOLLOW
Principle #2: Hope

*For I know the plans I have for you, declares
the LORD, plans to prosper you and not
to harm you, plans to give you hope and a
future.*

Jeremiah 29:11 NIV

In my work with women recovering from eating disorders, I occupy a role which I have come to believe is nothing less than sacred. I am a hope-holder for others. By the time most women have arrived in residential treatment for their eating disorder (or substance abuse, PTSD, mood disorder, etc), they have very little hope remaining, and they have likely lost their ability to envision a life of freedom for themselves. Enter the Treatment Team, a unity of individual clinicians working together alongside the individual, to help her find the path to freedom. She needs us to guide her, to support her, to encourage her, to challenge her, but perhaps the most important thing we do for any woman walking through our doors is to hold the hope when hers is lost, until she finds it once again.

Hope is a must in recovery. Without hope, why bother? Hope is the unwavering belief that something better lies ahead. What is your "something better?" A life free of the fear, compulsions, and entrapment of your eating disorder? A life in which you can enjoy an outing to the beach, an ice cream with friends on a summer night, or moving your body for the sheer pleasure of it? Maybe for you in this moment, you simply hope for a life in which you will wake up in the morning and be grateful to be alive, because maybe, just maybe, you've forgotten what it really *means* to be alive.

Hope is essential. You simply have to have it or surround yourself with those who have it for you, for the time being, but it must be built upon something real. Today's scripture passage reveals the heart of God toward His chosen ones. (Yes, Beautiful, that's you!) He has plans for us. For me. For you. Good plans. Exciting plans. Secret plans that He longs to reveal to us as time unfolds and we walk with Him in faith. Do you believe that? Is it possible that God isn't finished with you yet? Is it possible (can you dare to allow yourself to believe, even for a moment) that perhaps the best is yet to come?

Precious woman, you were made for more than this. You were not created for defeat, but for victory—a victory that God made possible for you through Jesus; a victory that has already been purchased and paid in full. The best *is* yet to come for you if you are willing to trust in God and follow as he leads. I believe that with everything inside me. I wouldn't dare put it in print if I didn't believe it with all my heart... for you.

Hope is not an option on this journey. You are going to need it. If you are without hope, I pray you borrow some from the pages of this book and from others around you as you accept their support and love. Better days, better years, a better life are ahead, dear one. Hold on.

FOOD FOR THOUGHT

1. Who are the hope-holders in your life? Consider writing or calling a few of them to express your thankfulness for the hope they carry on your behalf.

2. Are you able, in this moment, to take God at His word when he promises that His plans for you are good? If so, why? If not, what past hurts may be hindering your trust in His promises?

3. Do you believe the best is yet to come if you place your trust in God? What keeps you from living as though that were true?

4. In your journal, write out a prayer to God, asking Him to restore your hope one day at a time. If He has already begun to do so, thank Him for His restorative power at work in your heart.

God, I choose today to take You at Your word. Your plans for me are good, and You do not intend to harm me in any way. Because You are trustworthy, because You are love, I place my hope in You alone. May it grow each day as I draw nearer to You.

DAY 10: I SURRENDER ALL...AGAIN
Principle #3: Faith

*This is what the LORD says: Do not be
afraid! Don't be discouraged...for the battle
is not yours, but God's.*

2 Chronicles 20:15 NLT

I wish this were an easier devotion to write, I really do. But because I, too, have struggled with an eating disorder in my life, perfectionism and control seem to be built into me, just like they may seem to be built into you, and the concept of surrender has never come easily.

What kind of word pictures come to mind when you think of the word *surrender?* Do you think of a white flag waving in the air, signaling the end of battle? Do you picture two kids on either end of a rope, playing tug-of-war, and then one kid letting go of the rope, bending over exhaustedly and wiping her brow? For many years, I thought surrender meant to give up. And, never one to be a quitter, I didn't like that idea at all.

But imagine, if you will, a different image. Imagine one of those children playing tug-of-war, yanking and pulling so strenuously on her end of the rope that her hands are bleeding. Every time she thinks she gets a fresh, firm grasp on the rope, her opponent yanks a little harder and she loses it again then re-tightens her grasp, with an even more bloodied hand than before. She tries again with renewed resolve, but she is even weaker this time around because of her fresh wounds. Finally, after she can no longer stand the pain, instead of letting go and letting the rope simply fall, she cries out to God, "Take it!" And His able hand, firm and steady and strong, takes the rope from her and battles on her behalf, while His other hand holds her close to His chest and comforts her. The battle is still being fought. She hasn't given up, she has given *over*. And while the war continues, she knows that if she just stays close to Him, in the end she wins.

"Let go and let God" is a beautiful concept, but far more easily said than done. And why is that? Shouldn't giving our struggles to God and letting Him help us out come naturally to us? After all, why would we want to exhaust our own fallible strength when a wealth of unlimited, infallible power is available to us through God? Perhaps it has something to do with control. What if God doesn't fight in the same way we do? What if we can't see what He's doing and it looks like He will drop us? What if sometimes we can't feel Him pulling the rope for us, and we begin to fear He has let go?

You will feel this way, I assure you—sometimes more

often than not, especially if surrender is a new concept to you. When those days come, read today's scripture passage again. And then let go of your proverbial rope—again. God hasn't changed and He never will. The battle is still His, not yours. He's got you, and He is fighting on your behalf.

One more time: God's got this. Rest.

FOOD FOR THOUGHT

1. What pictures come to mind when you think of the word surrender?

2. Have you, too, thought that surrender meant giving up? In your own words, how would you explain the difference between giving *up* and giving *over*?

3. What would God have to promise you in order for you to surrender your eating disorder to Him with confidence?

4. Re-read today's scripture. When read in context, this passage is referring to an actual war being waged against a mighty army. How is your eating disorder like a war? How will you know when you are unable to fight it on your own?

Father, I am tired; You did not create me to fight on my own apart from You. I admit my powerlessness to You, and I confess that I've tried for too long to fight this battle in my own strength. I need You, but giving up control is difficult for me.

Thank You that You know my heart and its deepest fears and apprehensions. I rest in You today, knowing that You are fighting on my behalf. Just for today, I surrender all to You and I trust that You will give me the grace to do the same tomorrow.

DAY 11: TAKE COURAGE!
Principle #4: Courage

Haven't I commanded you? Strength!
Courage! Don't be timid; don't get
discouraged. GOD, your God, is with you
every step you take.

Joshua 1:9 MSG

What comes to mind when you think of the word courageous? Typical images might include a firefighter charging into a burning building to save those trapped inside, or the stone-faced resolve of an armed soldier marching into battle, or perhaps a woman in labor, being wheeled toward the delivery room, gripping the rails of the hospital bed and saying, "Let's do this!"

Why do those people do such things? Why does the firefighter deliberately walk into flames? Why does the soldier march directly toward an enemy after his blood? Why does the weary mother-to-be reach deep within herself to some secret reservoir of strength and determine that she will not relent despite her incredible exhaustion? Where do they get such courage? And, how can you?

Courage is a recurring theme in scripture. In fact, the most repeated command to us in the Bible is to "fear not." And Jesus Himself can be quoted multiple times in the New Testament telling others to "take courage" (Matthew 9:2; John 16:33). Courage, then, is something we *take,* not something we *feel.* It is a resource available to us and He invites us to take it as needed.

Do you need a dose of courage today? If you're battling an eating disorder, you surely do. Your specific need of courage may vary from moment to moment. You may need courage to follow your meal plan or to stay away from the bathroom for an hour after each meal, or to go to therapy and explore painful truths about yourself, your past, your family, etc. Recovery is a treacherous uphill journey at times. You will need courage in your backpack.

The firefighter runs into the flames because the survival of others depends upon his courage. The soldier risks his life in battle because freedom depends upon his courage. The laboring mother summons an inner stamina she didn't even know she had because her courage will bring forth new life. Lives depend upon courage.

Your life, dear sister, depends upon courage. And your God has gone before you to make a way. He is with you every step you take. Take courage! There is not a single step in this journey that you will ever have to take alone.

FOOD FOR THOUGHT

1. On a scale of one to ten, ten being fearless and one being terrified, how courageous do you feel today?

2. Good news: Courage is not a feeling. Courage is something you *take*. What does that mean, in your own words?

3. Name one thing you face today in your recovery for which you need to take courage.

4. Write out a prayer in your journal, asking God to give you the courage you need for today. Remember that it is His pleasure to empower you with what you need as you draw your strength from Him.

God, sometimes as I battle my eating disorder, it feels as though it is stronger than I am, and I am scared to do the right thing. I need You, and I need the courage that only You can give me. I am weak and frightened apart from You, but I choose to remind myself that with You, I can do all things. I will not be discouraged today.

DAY 12: WITH ALL MY HEART
Principle #5: Integrity

*He is a double-minded man, unstable in all
he does.*

James 1:8 NIV

Integrity can be defined several ways, such as: "The quality of possessing and steadfastly adhering to high moral principles or professional standards" or "firm adherence to a code of especially moral or artistic values." But perhaps the most applicable definition of the word integrity, for our benefit in our recovery journey, is the very simplest definition. Integrity can also be defined as: "Wholeness, completeness, the state of being complete or undivided."

For a woman recovering from an eating disorder, the state of being undivided may sound utterly foreign and unimaginable. When we are ensnared by anorexia or bulimia, we are undoubtedly divided between a desire for health and a desire for the comfort of sickness; between a resolve to refrain from restricting or purging and a resolve to control our weight and our food at all costs; between a deceptive drive to obey and please the false god of our eating disorder and an innate, God-given desire to do what pleases Him (Philippians 2:13). This sort of double-mindedness is emotionally exhausting. And, while the state of being undivided may sound foreign to us, it probably also sounds absolutely wonderful—if only we could get there.

So how do we do it? How do we re-program years of faulty thinking? How do we get ourselves in line with God's way of thinking and practice living that way until it becomes natural and automatic? How does an ambivalent woman achieve such a state of integrity? Is it even possible?

If it is our goal to become more and more like Jesus, to reflect our Creator more clearly each day, to be imitators of God (Ephesians 5:1), then I believe it is possible. Easy? No. Possible? Yes—eventually. Achieving integrity in our thinking, in our behavior, and in recovery will surely be a process, just like everything else. Few things in our faith-walk ever happen instantly. Have you ever noticed that? Sometimes that frustrates those of us who deal with rigidity and perfectionism. We want to be good, and we want it now!

Thankfully, God does not approach us with the same demanding rigidity as we approach ourselves. He knows what we are. He knows that He made us from the dust of the ground and most of us are not exactly a quick study when it comes to learning to be like Jesus. He seems to be okay with that, though. In fact, He must enjoy walking us through the process, or He would have made us capable of instant holiness. He certainly could have if He had wanted it to be that way. If we could snap our fingers and take our children from birth to young adulthood, we would certainly save time and headaches along the way, but we wouldn't have the joy of watching them grow. God, too, seems to enjoy the maturing process, perhaps because it is the process by which we grow in relationship with Him. Letting Him grow us up is how we get to know Him.

So how do we do that? Thankfully, like any good parent, God instructs us along the way. His Word is rich with instruction for living, all of which, when read and studied and applied and practiced (again and again and again), will refine us into women of integrity. Search your Bible and see what jumps out at you today. He may tell you to cast your anxiety on Him (1 Peter 5:7), or to take captive every thought to make it obedient to Christ (2 Corinthians 10:5), or to renew your mind with His word so that He might transform you (Romans 12:2). Ask the Spirit of God to show you today what instruction He would have you practice as you make wholeness and completeness your goal. I assure you, He will speak.

FOOD FOR THOUGHT

1. What might the state of being complete or undivided look like in your recovery and in your life? How would your days be different if you were truly able to live that way?

2. Do you often wish you could snap your fingers and *instantly* be a woman of integrity, or are you grateful that God seems to enjoy the process of growing us up?

3. Read Ephesians 5:1. What do you suppose it might mean to be an imitator of God?

4. Ask the Spirit of God to show you today what instruction He would have you practice as you make wholeness and completeness your goal. Use your journaling space to write this out as a prayer.

Father God, thank You for Your patience with me as I continue to practice living a life of integrity. I trust You, Lord, to work in me and to grow me into a woman who imitates You in all that I do. Thank You for gently instructing me, helping me to become whole and complete.

DAY 13: IF YOU ARE WILLING ...
Principle #6: Willingness

*A man with leprosy came and knelt in
front of Jesus, begging to be healed. 'If you
are willing, you can heal me and make me
clean,' he said. Moved with compassion,
Jesus reached out and touched him. 'I am
willing,' he said. 'Be healed!'*

Mark 1:40-41 NLT

I love the story of the leper's healing in Mark,
chapter one. When I read this story, I get a mental picture
of Jesus' face lighting up in a brilliant smile, love shining
in His twinkling eyes as He takes the sick man's face in His
holy, soon-to-be-scarred hands, enthusiastically proclaiming
His willingness to make the man clean and whole. In my
interpretation, He might as well have responded, "Are you
kidding me? You bet I'm willing! I want the very best for
you—and besides, your faith is blowing me away right now.
I love that about you!"

It wasn't a question of Jesus' willingness at all. Rather, the sick man's healing depended upon his own willingness— his willingness to admit his need, to ask for healing, and to dare to believe that Jesus would receive him. The leper was willing to do these things because he wanted health. He wanted to be clean and whole. And he wanted it *bad*.

God is willing to make us whole, to free us from the diseases and disorders that have enslaved us to lives of fear and shame. We need not even ask Him if it is His will for us to be free of our eating disorders. Eating disorders are rooted in shame and deception, and God is light and truth. His desire to see us free of our diseases is a no-brainer. After all, "it was for freedom that Christ has set us free" (Galatians 5:1), and "whom the Son sets free is free indeed" (John 8:36).

God is willing for us to be made whole. The question is, are we?

Willingness is an essential recovery principle in the battle against an eating disorder. And in theory, we might say, "Sure, God, I'm willing. Go ahead and fix me. Take it away. Let me wake up tomorrow feeling and thinking differently, and then I will behave differently." If only it worked that way. But there's more to the question when God is the one doing the asking. "Are you willing to follow Me, even when you don't know where I'm leading you? Are you willing to trust Me? (Okay, and let's get real: Are you willing to trust your dietician? Your therapist? Your psychiatrist?) Are you willing to let go of the control that you have come to believe will keep you safe? Are you willing to surrender?"

Whoa! Those are tough questions, aren't they? And you may have answered them rather passionately, whether your answer was yes or no. What feelings do these questions awaken in you? Fear? Anxiety? Anger? Ambivalence? If so, dear sister, you may have a willingness problem. But take heart; God already knows about it.

God looks upon your heart. He knows where you are in terms of willingness in your recovery process. What's most important today is that *you* know where you are. And now that you know, you can take the next step. Talk with God about it.

FOOD FOR THOUGHT

1. Do you believe God is willing to make you clean? Have you ever questioned this? Why or why not?

2. Re-read the fourth paragraph on page forty-six. Which of the "Are you willing?" questions is most difficult for you to answer honestly?

3. Was there ever a time when you found you were more willing and open to the recovery process than you are today? What has changed? What will it take for you to return to a place of greater willingness?

4. Use your journal to write out a prayer, confessing your willingness problem to God. Remember, He will not shame you for being where you are, so reject those accusing thoughts. God is

abounding in love and mercy (Psalm 103:8) toward you today.

Father, thank You for Your willingness to meet me where I am today, and for refusing to leave me here. Help me with my resistance and unwillingness. I trust that You will be gentle with me as I yield and surrender to You a little more each day.

DAY 14: I CAN'T...GOD CAN...I'LL LET HIM
Principle #7: Humility

Humble yourselves before the Lord, and He will lift you up.

James 4:10 NIV

As I've gotten older, I've learned an interesting paradox about life: The longer I live and the more I learn, the more I realize I have yet to learn. Similarly, I've noticed that the wisest people I know are those who remain open-handed and teachable—those who willingly and readily admit they don't know it all. Humility, it seems, is key to spiritual growth and wisdom.

A common misconception about humility, though, is that, in order to be humble, we must see ourselves as devalued. Notice that God calls us to *humble* ourselves, not to *degrade* ourselves. True humility, for the believer, recognizes that God is God and we are not. Apart from Him, we can do nothing, but in Him and through Him we can do all things (Philippians 4:13). A spirit of humility does not say, "I am a loser." Humility says, "I desperately need God." Humility does not insist we are the scum of the earth. There are no second-class citizens in the Kingdom of God. Humility, instead, acknowledges we have incredible value which is not contingent upon what we can do, but rather is rooted in who, and whose, we are.

Women with eating disorders tend to be perfectionistic, achievement-oriented individuals. There is a tendency to believe if we just try harder, push ourselves more, and discipline ourselves more harshly, we will succeed. We have approached control of our food and our bodies this way, resulting in illness and disorder. Often we attempt to approach recovery with the same false belief that we can achieve our goals in our own strength and power if we just dig in and apply ourselves. This belief sets us up for failure because we cannot (and were not designed to) overcome in our own strength. We were created to be complete, whole, and victorious in the Lord, and not apart from Him.

Humility, then, does not simply say, "I can't." Humility says, "I can't, God can, and I choose to let Him lift me up." And we find in recovery, as in life, when we humble ourselves before a loving and sovereign God, it is His delight to exalt us to heights we never could have achieved or even imagined on our own.

FOOD FOR THOUGHT

1. What are some misconceptions you may have had about what it means to be humble?

2. What is the difference between humbling yourself and degrading yourself?

3. What is one way you can choose to remain open-handed and teachable today?

4. Use your journal to write out a prayer to God, asking Him to reveal to you what it means to humble yourself before Him in the context of recovery from your eating disorder.

Father, it is not easy for me to admit my weakness and need. I admit that apart from You, I can do nothing, but through You, I can do all things, for nothing is impossible for You. Lead me today as I look to You for guidance in all that I do.

DAY 15: KEEP ON KEEPIN' ON
Principle #8: Discipline/Perseverance

Consider it pure joy, my brothers and sisters,
whenever you face trials of many kinds,
because you know that the testing of your
faith produces perseverance. Let perseverance
finish its work so that you may be mature
and complete, not lacking anything.

James 1:2-4 NIV

In October of 1941, Winston Churchill gave a commencement speech for the students at his alma mater, the Harrow School. It is still quoted today. In fact, not only is it often quoted, many have the abbreviated version of the speech committed to memory:

"Never, never, never give in!" Or give up!

Poetic, isn't it? Reportedly, Mr. Churchill articulated this brief speech from the podium, gaining volume and intensity with each word, and then sat right back down.

Clearly, he meant what he said. It's okay to be a man of few words when the words carry that much passion.

What about you? Are you passionate about persevering in recovery from your eating disorder? Are you committed to never, never, never giving up? Notice, if you will, what Winston Churchill did not say. He did not say:

"Never, never, never mess up!"

No one would print that on a T-shirt or mug, now would they? No way. And why not? Because perseverance does not mean perfection.

If you are struggling with an eating disorder, chances are you already live under the self-imposed pressure of perfectionism. Let me help you out. Perfection is a myth; an unattainable ideal that will keep you forever spinning on a proverbial hamster's wheel, never to reach your unrealistic goal. Cruel, isn't it?

Mistakes are allowed. Mess-ups are allowed. And, dare I say it? Relapse is allowed. It is acceptable to fall, but choose to fall forward. And what does that mean in your battle against ED? It means getting up after a fall, persevering day after day, one day at a time, one meal at a time, one bite at a time.

Let's be real, sister. Where did perfectionism get you? It landed you in the snare of your eating disorder. It became a disease. It fooled you and it betrayed you. And guess what? Your recovery will not be perfect. It *can't* be perfect. You cannot cure perfectionism *with* perfectionism.

So, what do you do? Expect mistakes. Accept mess-ups. And never, never, never give up!

FOOD FOR THOUGHT

1. How has perfectionism played a role in your eating disorder, or in its development?

2. How might perfectionism threaten to hinder your progress in recovery?

3. What is your usual reaction to having made a mistake in recovery?

4. You cannot cure perfectionism with perfectionism. Do you agree? Why or why not?

Father God, I confess that my desire to do things perfectly often distracts me from my recovery goals, and I am often tempted to give up after a fall. Please help me to accept the imperfect nature of my recovery journey, and give me daily strength to keep on keepin' on. I trust You to get me where I am going. Bless my imperfect efforts, leading me into Your perfect will.

DAY 16: DON'T DRINK THE POISON!
Principle #9: Forgiveness

For if you forgive men when they sin against you, your Heavenly Father will also forgive you.

Matthew 6:14 NIV

The principle of forgiveness is a difficult one for many people, especially those who have been abused, neglected, or violated. And sadly, a great many of those with eating disorders fit that description. It's one thing to forgive the woman who cut you off on the freeway, for example, but how do you forgive a parent who abandoned you? Or an abuser who violated your most basic human rights? Or perhaps the most difficult person for an addict of any kind to forgive—how do you forgive yourself?

If I could, I would tell you that you could pick and choose whom to forgive and to what extent. I would tell you partial, selective forgiveness is good enough. But if our scripture passage is true (and all scripture is), that would mean our Heavenly Father could measure out our own forgiveness similarly—that such as we forgive, so too would we be forgiven. And I don't know about you, but I need total forgiveness, absolute pardon, over and over and over again. I'm just not perfect enough for anything else. Are you?

Forgiveness is not something we can get out of. There simply aren't any loopholes. But that's only half the truth. Thankfully, the larger part is that our call to forgiveness is an invitation from our loving Father, who tenderly holds our best interest at heart—always. God invites us to a life and a lifestyle of forgiveness, because when we walk in forgiveness and mercy toward ourselves and others, we let go of the bitterness that would otherwise ensnare us (Hebrews 12:14-15). The more tightly we hold on to a grudge, the more tightly that grudge holds *us*.

When we hold on to grudges and harbor bitterness and resentment in our heart toward others, *we* are the ones who suffer. In fact, it has been said that holding onto resentment and refusing to forgive an offender is like drinking poison and then waiting for the other person to die. Usually, the other person will go about his or her life, largely unaware of the unrest we have chosen to invite into our hearts by not releasing them into the hands of God and allowing *Him* to avenge us. In other words, forgiveness really isn't for the benefit of the offender so much as it is for *us*. In fact, forgiveness actually unleashes us from the control that our offenders might otherwise have in our lives.

Free of the root of bitterness, we become able to live open-hearted and open-handed, seeing others as God sees them, and as God sees us: fallible, broken humanity in need of love. And without a root of bitterness choking the life out of our hearts, we abandon ourselves to love others, to love God, and to love ourselves.

FOOD FOR THOUGHT

1. Do you find it more difficult to forgive others or to forgive yourself? Why?

2. The more tightly you hold on to a grudge, the more tightly that grudge holds you. What does this mean, in your own words?

3. Do you agree with that statement (in the question above)? Why or why not?

4. In your journal, write out a simple prayer, asking the Spirit of God to show you anywhere you might have allowed a root of bitterness to grow in your heart. Ask Him to reveal to you one specific person toward whom He would ask you to extend forgiveness.

Father, You know the hurts and wounds in my heart. You are aware of my pain and still You ask me to forgive. I ask You, in Your mercy, to enable me to walk in forgiveness and mercy toward others, recognizing that forgiveness is a choice of my will and not of my emotions. Lord, I will not wait to "feel like" forgiving that person You have brought to my attention; rather, I choose today to forgive because I myself am forgiven.

DAY 17: WHY ASK WHY?
Principle #10: Acceptance

If you do this, you will experience God's peace, which is far more wonderful than the human mind can understand. His peace will guard your hearts and minds as you live in Christ Jesus.

Philippians 4:7 NLT

Say it with me, girls. I know you know it by heart: "God, grant me the serenity to accept the things I cannot change, the courage to change the things I can, and the wisdom to know the difference."

I don't know about you, but the first part of that prayer is the hardest for me. I don't generally hesitate to change those things over which I have power. Change is action and action feels like control, and frankly, I like that. (Can I get an *Amen?*) As for the wisdom to know the difference between the changeable and unchangeable, well, that usually comes through trial and error. But that acceptance part—it feels a bit...*passive.* Doesn't it?

That's what I used to think. To me, acceptance used to feel a bit like defeat. Acceptance, I mistakenly thought, was a deep sigh...a shrug of the slumped, rounded shoulders...a dramatic and melancholy, "Oh, well." Who wants to embrace that as a principle of recovery?

But, alas, I was mistaken. In years of practicing acceptance (and by practicing, I mean messing up and starting over again and again and again), I have learned the truth: Acceptance, as we mean to apply it to our eating disorder recovery journey, is anything but passive. On the contrary, acceptance—the kind of peaceful, trusting acceptance that God gives us grace to operate in—is empowering.

There are many, many things in this world and in our lives that we cannot change. We cannot go back and re-write history. We cannot unsay regrettable things we have said. We cannot always reverse the consequences our diseases have had on our lives and on the lives of others. We cannot delete the parts of our life story we wish had never taken place, like trauma or tragedy or loss. And when we choose not to ask God for the grace to accept those things, we are left with one burning question, eating us alive from the inside out: "Why?"

Why was I abused? Why did my mother/father/ boyfriend/husband leave me? Why did my loved one have to die? Why was I so foolish to make the bad choices I made? Why did I end up fighting this eating disorder battle when

Hope For The Hollow

so many others around me have come through their lives seemingly unscathed? Why, why, why?

Here's the problem with "why." There isn't always an answer for it. And what then? What if the whys in our lives are destined, and perhaps even designed, to remain unanswered this side of heaven? What if only God Himself has those answers, and what if He decides, as only He is authorized to decide, that they are not ours to be had? Or what if we are not yet ready to handle those answers? How long will we continue to tread water, going nowhere, growing more and more bitter and jaded as we beg for answers from a God who will remain firmly, albeit lovingly and protectively, silent?

When we truly endeavor and purpose in our hearts to live out the Serenity Prayer, embracing acceptance as a way of life and yielded to the wisdom of God regardless of our ability to understand His ways, we free ourselves from the obsessive thinking of why, why, why? If a rejection of acceptance asks why, then acceptance asks a question of its own. Acceptance asks: "What now?" For example:

"I don't know why I was abused, God. I sure wish You had done something to stop that from happening. I believe You love me, and I know You wept with me and for me as those horrible events took place. Even though I may be angry and confused, and even though my pain is still present, I believe You will not waste my pain, but will use it to draw me closer to You. So, what now?"

Acceptance doesn't only apply to our biggest hurts and hurdles; acceptance is also the principle that will empower us to make it through our hours and days with victory, as well. It would be ever so easy to let minor annoyances like a bad hair day or a traffic jam or accidentally sleeping through the alarm ruin our day. "Ugh! Nothing ever goes right. I can't believe I did that. I am such an idiot! I might as well just give up on this day right now." Talk about a setup for failure. A morning like that, approached with that kind of stinking thinking, pretty much sets the stage for one of two things: a binge to comfort ourselves, or a day of restricting in an attempt to regain control and/or punish ourselves for "being such an idiot." Sound familiar?

Practicing the principle of acceptance, we might pray like this: "Okay, God. This morning sure is off to a rough start. Since I can't go back and start over, I choose to give this day to You. Only You can redeem a day like this. I am in a horrible mood and just feel like giving up. Please walk with me through this day. I need Your presence."

What a difference acceptance can make, both in the mundane hurdles of daily life and in the decades-deep wounds we may have allowed to arrest our development into godly women.

Acceptance promises peace, even if our circumstances do not (or can never) change. Acceptance, such as God enables us to lay hold of it, is a gift. It is ours for the taking.

FOOD FOR THOUGHT

1. Which part of the Serenity Prayer do you find

most challenging to put into practice? Why?

2. What a difference acceptance can make, both in the mundane hurdles of daily life and in the decades-deep wounds we may have allowed to arrest our development into godly women. In which area of your life/recovery do you find it most difficult to practice acceptance—the big things or the little things?

3. Do you relate to the scenario of the day that was off to a rough start? When have you recently experienced a situation in which your "stinking thinking" set   the tone for your whole day? What might you have done differently, and how might the result have been different if you had practiced acceptance?

4. Use your journal to write down three things you are currently struggling to accept, whether big things or little things. Truly, none of it is little to God. He cares. Write out a prayer asking Him to help you to accept those things so you might know His peace.

Father, I confess that I am not always quick to accept those things I cannot change. Help me to discern which things You are calling me to accept, and then meet me in my struggle, right where I am. Thank You for loving me, even in my stubbornness. Soften my heart today, Lord. I need You and I trust You.

DAY 18: GROWING PAINS
Recovery Principle #11: Knowledge and Awareness

When I was a child, I talked like a child, I thought like a child, I reasoned like a child. When I became a (wo)man, I put childish ways behind me.

1 Corinthians 13:11 NIV

As we dig deeper into recovery work, we have plenty of opportunities to grow in knowledge and wisdom. The more "heart work" we do in therapy or in treatment, the more we learn about our diseases and ourselves—why we do what we do, where certain tendencies or predispositions came from, and most importantly, we learn new tools to empower us to cope in healthier, more godly ways.

Here's the thing: God only expects us to walk in light of what we know, to live by the light we have thus far. But once we have new knowledge and revelation from Him, once

He has opened our eyes to new truth, we are responsible to walk in that truth. This, for the believer, is called growing up.

Do you remember what growing pains felt like? I can remember being about seven or eight years old and my legs would just ache and ache as I lay in bed at night trying to sleep. I used to ask my mom to grab me by the ankles and *pull*, thinking I could make the process happen a little more quickly. But growth only happens in God's time, as He sees fit. Ever notice that? We cannot rush the process, but we also cannot reverse it.

Sometimes it would be so much easier to just go back, wouldn't it? Turn the calendar pages back a few months or years to a time when we didn't know any better, or when God didn't seem to expect quite as much from us. I like what Mother Teresa said: "I know God will never give me more than I can handle. I just wish He didn't trust me so much."

Does God trust you? Has He been showing you things about yourself lately, trusting you with new knowledge and revelation? If so, sister, it sounds like God is growing you up, and growth hurts sometimes. Childhood is certainly easier than adolescence, and adolescence easier still than adulthood, but we cannot stay in puberty forever.

Your destiny awaits you as you walk in new knowledge and let God take you further. Will you trust Him and walk?

FOOD FOR THOUGHT

1. What might it mean for you to "put childish things behind you"? What is one way you can begin to do that today?

2. What is one new thing God has shown you about yourself so far in recovery? What has He shown you this week? Or just today?

3. Do you identify at all with Mother Teresa quote? How so?

4. Growing pains hurt. Rather than just grin and bear it, why not use your journal to tell God how you feel? (Note: Whining is permitted!) Tell the Lord what you are feeling and let His Spirit minister to your hurts. A loving father understands that growing up is hard.

Father, thank You for understanding my hesitation to grow. As You continue to entrust more knowledge to me, help me learn to walk in it. I trust You to nurture me through my growth process.

DAY 19: GRATITUDE ADJUSTMENT
Principle #12: Gratitude

Every good and perfect gift is from above, coming down from the Father of the Heavenly lights, who does not change like shifting shadows.

James 1:17 NIV

"Learn to live with an attitude of gratitude." We hear it so often it has become a cliché, and the danger with that is we often don't take it seriously or give much thought to what it really means. Attitude of gratitude. Not a moment of gratitude, not a day of gratitude, not a few passing grateful thoughts. An attitude. A mindset. A paradigm shift. A new way of seeing.

It is not always easy to be grateful, especially when our diseased minds are battling us for control over our thought life. "Grateful?" you might ask. "For what? I've had a difficult life. I'm plagued by traumatic memories. I have an eating disorder. I hate myself. And I'm supposed to be grateful?"

Well, yes. God calls us to gratitude. Not necessarily gratitude *for* our struggles (though, believe it or not, that may very well come later), but gratitude in spite of them and in the very midst of them.

"Is that even possible?" you ask. Of course it is. In fact, not only is a perspective of gratitude possible for you—right now, where you sit, as you are—but it is absolutely necessary and key to your recovery process.

Here's the thing about gratitude: Grateful people are hopeful people, because a grateful mindset knows if God has been faithful and good and has shown up in the past, chances are He's still good (since He never, ever changes) and He will show up again. In other words, intentionally remembering God's blessings in our lives naturally produces an expectancy of further blessing. Expecting good things nurtures hope, and hope is the key to recovery and restoration.

"But how do you do it? Where's the practical application? What are my action steps?"

Glad you asked. And you'll be happy to know, there is only one step to gratitude: choose it. Choose to be grateful. (Notice I didn't say choose to *feel* grateful; chose to *be* grateful.) Gratitude isn't a feeling; it's a decision, a choice.

What are you grateful for right now in this moment? Maybe the sun is shining or you slept well last night or you received a card in the mail. Maybe you got to see a good

Hope For The Hollow

friend today or you got a good parking spot at the store. It's okay to be grateful for the little things. Once we become treasure-hunters, intentionally seeking out the good, we find we don't have to look quite so hard.

Can't think of anything? If you woke up this morning, you have a very good reason to be grateful today. You've been given another chance at a meaningful life. So? What will you do with it?

FOOD FOR THOUGHT

1. Do you believe gratitude is a choice rather than a feeling? Why or why not?

2. Expecting good things nurtures hope, and hope is the key to recovery and restoration. Do you agree? What might it look like in your own life if you walked through each day expecting God to show you new things?

3. It is difficult to be purposeful about gratitude when our diseased minds are battling for control of our thoughts. How do you know when this is happening?

4. What can you do to regain control over your thoughts and return to gratefulness?

God, You have given me so many reasons to be grateful. Please forgive me for overlooking them at times. I often find myself blinded to the blessings You provide, and I don't want to miss out on opportunities to thank You. I ask You to open my eyes to blessings and teach me to be a treasure-seeker in my own life. Today, in my recovery and in my heart, I choose gratitude.

DAY 20: HELP A SISTER OUT

But encourage one another daily, as long as it is called today, so that none of you may be hardened by sin's deceitfulness.

Hebrews 3:13 NIV

Often when we are in the throes of our eating disorder, we can become susceptible to living life as though we had blinders on our eyes, aware only of ourselves and our all-consuming obsessions. Caught up in the web of our individual diseases and symptoms, we can lose sight of those around us who may also be experiencing pain or needs of their own.

A promising sign of our gradual emergence is when others begin to come into view and we are becoming well enough to reach out to them with words of love and encouragement. God's design and intention for us is to become interdependent, walking alongside one another in love and building one another up with encouragement from His word (1 Thessalonians 5:11).

A common mistake in early recovery is to become co-dependent rather than inter-dependent, assuming caretaking roles for those around us, taking on their burdens often to the exclusion of our own needs and responsibilities. The goal is not to assume or take on our sister's pain, but rather to encourage her to look to God as her source of strength and power, just as we are learning to do ourselves. In doing so, there is a splash-back effect. The very words we speak to build her up in the faith will, in turn, build us up and refresh us as well (Proverbs 11:25).

There is incredible power in the words we speak. The Bible tells us we have the power to speak either words of destruction or words of life, for the tongue has the power of life and death (Proverbs 18:21). We have opportunities every day to be a voice of godliness and life to other women in recovery, and we are called to pray for one another (James 5:16), confessing our sins, so that we might be healed.

As we turn our focus off of ourselves long enough to take notice of someone else's need for edification and encouragement, our perspective becomes enlarged. And, as we begin to see prayer answered on behalf of others in recovery, our view of God and His incredible faithfulness toward us grows.

Open your eyes, sister. Who in your circle of influence could use a phone call, an encouraging card or letter, or a word of prayer today? Reach out to that one in faith and love and wait expectantly on the Lord to show both of you His faithfulness. He will.

FOOD FOR THOUGHT

1. In the chaos of our disease, we often tend to go to extremes relationally. Have you developed a tendency either to become blinded to the needs of those around you or to take on more of others' burdens than you should?

2. How might achieving balance in your relationships with other women strengthen you and help you in recovery?

3. Who is one person God is placing on your heart for you to encourage today? How will you reach out?

4. In your journal, write out a prayer for that person. Be sure to leave some space so that you might return later and record the ways in which God honors and responds to your prayer on her behalf. As righteous women of God, our prayers are powerful and effective (James 5:16).

Father, thank You for the opportunities You give me to build others up with my words and my prayers. May I use my tongue to speak life to my sisters in recovery.

DAY 21: RECOVERY ISN'T THE GOAL

And I am certain that God, who began the good work within you, will continue his work until it is finally finished.

Philippians 1:6 NLT

In our first reading on day one, we learned that recovery itself is too vague a goal to aspire to achieve. Rather, recovery is the key to unlocking other dreams and goals for our meaningful lives. In my work with women recovering from eating disorders, I am always excited by the things they begin to discover as they ask themselves, "What will recovery release me into?"

I keep every email and letter I receive from the women I have worked with in treatment and as I flip through the thick book of collected notes, cards, and letters, I read accounts of those who have gone on to experience things they never dreamed possible when they were so tightly ensnared by their disease.

Guess what, Jena? I'm back in school and I am loving my classes!

I moved to Tennessee and bought a dog. And every morning when we take our walk at sunrise, I thank God that I am no longer too exhausted to leave the house, or too depressed to get out of bed. This is better!

I organized the first-ever walk in my town for Eating Disorder Awareness Week. I love the feeling of helping others.

I graduated from NYU last Spring and passed my licensing exam. I have a small caseload of clients, and I still can't believe I am working as a therapist. Who knew?

We are expecting our second baby in the Fall. It is amazing to be free to focus on the miracle of the life within me rather than on my changing body.

I know these women, and I'm here to tell you, there was a time when they never would have believed any of these things would be possible for them. They, possibly much like you, thought their eating disorders were all that remained of them, of their lives. Or, they'd grown tired of the charade of trying to look like they were truly living when, in fact, they were only going through the motions. And they didn't think life after ED was a reality to be found. But they found it.

What will *you* find on the other side of recovery?

FOOD FOR THOUGHT

1. Recovery itself is too vague a goal. Do you agree with this statement? Why or why not?

2. What has been your recovery goal, if you've made one, in the past? Has it been a vague goal or a specific goal? Explain.

3. Re-read the excerpts from the letters from women in recovery. What would you hope to write in a similar letter one year from now?

4. What would you hope to write five years from now?

Lord, it is sometimes difficult for me to imagine what recovery might look like in my life. Thank You for encouraging me to dream specific dreams. I believe that as I dare to become a possibility thinker, and as I stop underestimating Your power at work in my life, You will begin to grow new dreams and goals within me

DAY 22: NO WORRIES

Give your entire attention to what God is doing right now, and don't get worked up about what may or may not happen tomorrow. God will help you deal with whatever hard things come up when the time comes.

Matthew 6:34 MSG

"I'm freaking out," Anne said to me one morning at breakfast. "I'm nervous about the pancakes my dietician wants me to eat."

I surveyed Anne's tray and replied, "Am I missing something? It appears that you have cereal this morning. I don't see any pancakes."

Sighing in exasperation, Anne answered, "Not today; Friday. I will have pancakes on *Friday* morning."

"But it's only Monday," I said.

"I know," Anne replied. "I'm getting a head start on my worrying."

Do you know someone like Anne who worries days, weeks, or even months in advance? Are *you* like Anne? Sometimes it is easy to get ahead of ourselves in recovery and life in general. We worry about money, the future, our children, our relationships, our education, our careers, our reputations, our pasts, and, let's be real; with all of that to worry about, it might seem easier to fixate on our weight, the size of our jeans, and the number of calories in a pancake.

Leo Buscaglia once said, "Worry never robs tomorrow of its sorrow, it only saps today of its joy." He had a good point there, didn't he? Nothing steals our joy quite as quickly as getting caught up in worrying about the unknown. Worry becomes an all-consuming distraction, turning our focus away from those things we have power over in the moment. Worry keeps us from surrendering and easily traps us into circular, defeated thinking. I've heard it said that worry is like a rocking chair; it gives you something to do but it does not get you anywhere.

If you're looking for "something to do," why not swap worry for prayer? God seemed to know we humans would be prone to anxiety. His Word is rich with instruction directing us to pray when we are tempted to worry.

If you don't know what you're doing, pray to the Father. He loves to help. You'll get his help, and won't be condescended to when you ask for it. Ask boldly, believingly, without a second thought. People who 'worry their prayers' are like wind-whipped waves (James 1:5-7, MSG).

Give all your worries and cares to God, for he cares about you (1 Peter 5:7, NLT).

Don't worry about anything; instead, pray about everything. Tell God what you need, and thank him for all he has done (Philippians 4:6, NLT).

Laying worry aside is especially beneficial to us as we are working toward recovery. Can you imagine a life without worry? Just think of all the brain space you would free up for other things; things like prayer and meditation, focused therapy work, and service to others. Jesus knew what a distraction worry could be so He instructs us in Matthew 6 to "give our entire attention to what God is doing right now," rather than allowing our focus to get derailed by worry over things we cannot change. God is always up to something. He doesn't want us to miss out on experiencing Him moving in our lives today because we are already in tomorrow.

I'm certain Anne did not enjoy her cereal that morning. How could she enjoy Monday's cereal when she was already focused on Friday's pancakes? Each moment that passes is a moment we will never get back. There are no second chances when it comes to time.

Don't waste your *now* worrying about *later*. Cast your anxiety on the Lord. Pray without ceasing. Make your requests known to Him. And then, sit back and enjoy your breakfast!

FOOD FOR THOUGHT

1. Do you know someone like Anne who worries in advance? Do you?

2. What does chronic worrying accomplish or give you? Is there a reward? Why do you suppose you do it?

3. Winston Churchill once said: "When I look back on all the worries, I remember the story of the old man who said on his deathbed that he had a lot of trouble in his life, most of which never happened." Can you think of something you spent a great deal of time worrying over, only to find that it never happened after all?

4. In your journal, make a list of the things that are currently worrying you the most. Then, one by one, give those anxieties to the Lord in prayer. If you are so inclined, create a "prayer box" to place your written worries in as they arise. Once you give them to God, leave them there!

Father, I know you are aware of my tendency to worry rather than to pray. Help me to remember your teachings about worry, and help me to bring all of my worries and anxieties to you daily. I trust that as I give you my anxiety, you will give me Your peace.

DAY 23: REPROGRAMMING

*Do not conform any longer to the pattern
of this world, but be transformed by the
renewing of your mind.*

Romans 12:2 NIV

Human beings are very easily influenced. We teach our children to talk mainly by talking in front of them. The children listen, assimilate our language, and begin to say what they hear us saying. By surrounding a child with information we want him to absorb, we influence him to learn our ways.

Another case in point: accents and dialects. My friend Cindy, who lost her life to bulimia, was from Fort Worth, Texas. Because we lived many miles apart, we grew our friendship by spending hours on the telephone with one another. Midwestern friends could always tell when I had spent an evening on the phone with Cindy, and would tease me about my easily-adopted drawl: "Come on back north, Jena; Chicago girls don't say *y'all!*" By immersing myself in conversation with Cindy, I unconsciously began to take on her characteristics.

The point? What we immerse ourselves in and surround ourselves with determines what we learn and internalize. For example, have you ever paid attention to how you feel or think about yourself after flipping through the pages of a fashion magazine? Digitally enhanced and airbrushed images of unrealistically thin and "perfect" women do not help me at all to approach myself and my body with gentleness and gratitude. Give me just fifteen minutes with those images and I begin to actually expect myself to measure up to those ridiculous retouched photos. If I'm not purposeful about telling myself the truth, I could easily close the glossy cover of a magazine and walk away convinced I am too short, too heavy, too wrinkled or oily or pimply, that my nails are ugly and imperfect, that my teeth could probably be whiter, that I need all new clothes, a new haircut, and depending on the magazine, maybe even a little plastic surgery!

That is what the world would have me believe. A lot of money is made every single day on women like you and me, who can so easily become conformed to "the pattern of this world," which brainwashes us into believing that: A) We are flawed; B) Perfection is not only possible, but the only acceptable standard; and C) We must chase after that standard with all of our might, all of our mind, and all of our money.

It's time for reprogramming. And according to our

scripture for today, we do that by renewing our mind with God's word. Our Father has made His opinion of us very clear in His word. It is His opinion—and not the shallow, shaming messages of this world and culture—that defines our value. The Word tells us that we are *fearfully and wonderfully made* (Psalm 139:14), that we are *God's masterpiece* (Ephesians 2:10), that we are created in God's image (Genesis 1:27), etc. And there is plenty more where that came from; we need only open our Bibles (instead of a fashion magazine) and look. (Sure. Try it!)

It is ever so easy to be a conformist, learning to think like the world, talk like the world, and obey the demands and expectations of the world. Seeking God's message instead of the world's message takes a bit more effort, but it is time well spent if we truly wish to reprogram our thinking.

FOOD FOR THOUGHT

1. In what ways have you conformed to the pattern of this world?

2. How have these beliefs played a role in the development (or exacerbation) of your eating disorder?

3. From your perspective, what are some of the world's messages that women must combat daily with true messages from the word of God?

4. Expressive art idea: Cut out various phrases, photos, etc. from a fashion magazine which

communicate the messages you listed in the question above and create a collage with them. On the reverse side of your collage, create an artistic collection of true messages from God's Word. Which "side" will you choose to believe?

God, all truth is Your truth. The patterns of this world are counterfeits and distractions from the true messages that You want me to believe. Help me to renew my mind daily with Your Word. As I immerse myself in Your truth, I trust that You will reprogram my mind to readily believe what You say about me.

DAY 24: TIMELESS BEAUTY

Charm is deceptive, and beauty is fleeting;
but a woman who fears the Lord is to
be praised.

Proverbs 31:30 NIV

I have been blessed to have several role models in my life who are amazing; godly women—women who truly are "to be praised." I look at them in wonder and awe at times. Just being around these women is inspirational to me. I like to look at their hands—hands that have fed many and nurtured children and served others in countless ways, not the least of which has been by folding in prayer for those whom they love.

Each woman I consider to be my role model is over the age of sixty, which some would consider to be past one's prime according to this world's standard of beauty. But these women, to me, are indescribably beautiful. And no one will convince me otherwise.

As our scripture passage states, beauty—physical, aesthetic beauty, such as defined by the world and particularly by our western culture—is fleeting. As I once heard a man say to his son on the son's wedding day, "If you like the way she looks today, well...take pictures." Dear ol' Dad may have been a bit shallow and jaded, but he had a point: No woman stays in her prime forever.

So why, then, are my godly role models so incredibly beautiful, even after six decades on the planet? What ineffable quality illuminates their faces, brightens their smiles, and causes them to carry themselves with such swagger and style and grace? What is it about them? And were they born with it?

No, I don't think so. I do not believe these ladies "came this way." I think their beauty was grown, seasoned, and earned. What is most stunning about them is their assurance. There seems to be a certain undeniable glow that comes from knowing better. It says: "I've been through some stuff. I've earned these laugh lines, these silver hairs. I've put in my time and I've learned that God can be trusted to take me through all my days, all my years, all my life. I have tasted and seen that the Lord is good" (Psalm 34:8).

And just being around them makes me want to taste and find out for myself.

FOOD FOR THOUGHT

1. Do you have older women in your life who fear the Lord and are to be praised? List them by name.

2. List the qualities about them which you find most attractive and/or beautiful.

3. Do you agree that beauty, by the world's standard, is fleeting? How do you feel about that truth? Can you accept the finite nature of worldly beauty?

4. Choose one or more of the women you listed in Question #1 and write her a short note or card telling her what she means to you and what beauty you see in her. Pray for that woman as you drop the card in the mail.

Father, thank You for these women in my life who fear You. I pray that You bless each of them today and show them their true, lasting beauty. Teach me to fear You, too, so that my own true beauty will never fade. I want to be praiseworthy because of my love for You.

DAY 25: SELF-SABOTAGE

Yes. I'm full of myself—after all, I've spent a long time in sin's prison. What I don't understand about myself is that I decide one way, but then I act another, doing things I absolutely despise. So if I can't be trusted to figure out what is best for myself and then do it, it becomes obvious that God's command is necessary.

Romans 7:15-17 MSG

This scripture passage was paraphrased from the book of Romans, but it might as well have been copied right out of some of our diaries. Why do we do what we don't want to do? Why do we promise ourselves and others that we will "be good"—stop purging, follow our meal plans, practice moderation in our physical activity, take our meds, whatever—and then turn right around and do the opposite of what we've purposed in our heart to do?

I once worked with a young woman in treatment whose self-sabotaging behavior was as predictable as a tornado.

I could see it coming, see the signs. She would set certain goals for herself, like achieving one week without purging, and something would always happen during the last meal of day *six* that she would choose to be her trigger, setting her off to use behaviors and break her winning streak. It took some time, but once we were able to identify these patterns, she got the support she needed to push through those high-stakes moments and achieve her goals, one at a time.

Do you have a tendency to sabotage yourself in recovery? Many of us do. When things start to fall in line and run smoothly for a little while, somewhere inside we, or our eating disorders, panic. We either create chaos, surround ourselves with temptation, or set ourselves up in some other way. And the tricky part is we seldom realize we are doing it.

God has a plan for you and He has gone before you and made a way out of your eating disorder. Often we fall into a pattern of thinking that would have us believe God is a distant scorekeeper, peering at us over his glasses to see if we're doing everything right. That kind of perception keeps us forever looking over our shoulder, afraid we're being graded, and afraid we're failing.

Chew on this: If we are trying to do this recovery thing in our own strength, failure is inevitable. That's the bad news, and the cold, hard truth. But there's good news too. If we continually decide we are going to do just one right thing at a time, and if we remain aware that it is not our strength but *God's* strength in which we operate, failure is impossible.

God wants you to win. He is your biggest fan, your loudest cheerleader, and the most compassionate counselor you will ever have on your team. He is not ticking off red checkmarks on your recovery report card. In fact, there is no report card. There are no grades. Think of it: If God is perfect and holiness is His standard, and all of us fall short of that standard, what curve could He possibly grade us on that wouldn't automatically flunk us all?

You are not being graded. It can be good to set goals for yourself in recovery. Milestones are important, but they are important to us, not to God. We celebrate milestones and sobriety anniversaries because *we* need the encouragement, not because God needs proof that we are still "being good." Remember: He sees our heart. He knows our intentions, whether good or bad. So when you get close to meeting a goal and you somehow unconsciously throw yourself off-track, know this: you are far more disappointed in yourself than God could ever be.

God is not disappointed in you when you *do what you don't want to do* (Romans 7:15 NIV). He is sad for you and He hurts with you, but He remains full of grace toward you, full of love, forgiveness, kindness, and mercy. God allows do-overs and it is His hope that when you do it over another time, you will be all the more aware of your weakness so that you might learn to rely upon His strength.

No shame. No grades. No judgment. Just love and mercy and restoration for a fresh start. You didn't *really* think you could do this on your own, did you?

FOOD FOR THOUGHT

1. Read over our scripture for today. If you have the means, try reading Romans 7 in a few different Bible translations. Which words or phrases stand out to you or grab you? Can you identify with the writer's frustration?

2. Have you ever thought of God as a distant scorekeeper? Do you still perceive Him that way? Why or why not?

3. Have you been trying to do recovery in your own strength? How do you know?

4. What can you do today to show God, and yourself, that you recognize your need for Him? How will you operate in God's strength as you take on this day?

God, I can't do this on my own. No matter how hard I try to do good and to be good, I always seem to mess myself up somehow. I realize that I need You in order to fight and win this battle against my eating disorder, or any other battle that arises in my life. In my own strength, failure in inevitable, but when I operate in Your strength, failure is impossible. Thank You for the reminder today.

DAY 26: THE ONLY WAY OUT IS THROUGH

Consider it a sheer gift, friends, when tests and challenges come at you from all sides. You know that under pressure, your faith-life is forced into the open and shows its true colors. So don't try to get out of anything prematurely. Let it do its work so you become mature and well-developed, not deficient in any way.

James 1:2-4 MSG

I once worked with a young woman in treatment whom I nicknamed "Loophole" because she always looked for an easy way out, seeking the path of least resistance. I tried not to laugh too loudly the day she said to me, "I want to recover; I do. I don't mind doing the work in therapy. I'm just not willing to feel any emotions, that's all."

Loophole's statement might sound laughable and ironic, but I think many of us think this way at times in the context of recovery. "I will do *this* and *this*, but not *that*. I want to *be* there; I just don't want to have to *get* there. Wake me up when I reach wherever it is I am going. It is the *journey* I wish to avoid."

I'll tell you exactly what I told Loophole that day: The only way out is through. Most people aren't given honorary degrees; they have to actually go to college and study for four years. A musician doesn't rent a student violin on Friday and show up at Carnegie Hall on Saturday. He practices for years and hones his skill. Anything truly worth achieving is worth working for. Is recovery worth the effort of the journey to you?

There are no loopholes in recovery work—no fast track, no accelerated study program, no get-out-of-jail-free-card to play. It must be walked out, one step at a time, one day at a time, one meal at a time, and one moment of abstinence followed by another, followed by another. *Line upon line, precept upon precept* (Isaiah 28:10). In other words, little by little.

Recovery from an eating disorder, especially one that has gone on for many years, as was the case with Annie (she doesn't go by Loophole anymore), takes time. It takes work; years of work—cumulative work, faithful work, covered in prayer. After a while, you begin to enjoy the scenery. You learn to stop focusing on your desire for a quick fix or a sudden rescue and you start to take the journey as it comes. And one day you stop, turn around, and say, "How did You get me here, Lord?"

As you look over your shoulder at the ground you've covered, you will know what Annie has learned...a lesson so life-changing she has since had it tattooed on the inside of her wrist: "The only way out is through."

FOOD FOR THOUGHT

1. Are you like Loophole, always looking for an easy way out? What is something you might be trying to get out of prematurely in your recovery journey right now?

2. If the only way out is through, is it worth it to you to persevere through the journey of recovery? Why or why not?

3. What is another goal in your life you have achieved little by little? How did you remain focused during the process?

4. How might rushing through recovery work hinder you long-term?

Lord God, I admit my impatience to You today. Sometimes I would like to be able to snap my fingers and be at the end of this recovery journey. Thank You for your patience with me, even when I do not have patience with You or with the process You are taking me through. I will not rush my recovery. I trust You to lead me out of my eating disorder, little by little.

DAY 27: SHHH...REST

Are you tired? Worn out? Burned out on religion? Come to me. Get away with me and you'll recover your life. I'll show you how to take a real rest. Walk with me and work with me—watch how I do it. Learn the unforced rhythms of grace. I won't lay anything heavy or ill-fitting on you. Keep company with me and you'll learn to live freely and lightly.

Matthew 11:28-30 MSG

A real rest? What is that, exactly? For those of us who struggle with eating disorders, the idea of rest may have become unclear over time, as our disease so ruthlessly dictates to us how we spend our hours and days. When was the last time you truly experienced what it was like to "rest in the Lord"? Have you ever had such an experience?

Somewhere in our past, many of us forgot what it meant to be a human being and we became "human doings."

Go, go, go, go, go. Sound familiar? Afraid of silence and stillness, we created lives of frantic activity from morning until night. Whether we spent our days anxiously obsessing over our work, studying endlessly in our pursuit of academic perfection, or simply doing whatever it took to stay in constant motion, chances are that we have conditioned ourselves not to prioritize rest.

God created within us an innate longing for rest. We crave it physically, emotionally, and spiritually. And beyond our body's physiological need for restorative down time (it's called sleep, remember?), God created us to long for time with Him spent resting in His presence. His Spirit is forever waiting on us to sit with Him, talk with Him, and be still enough to listen.

Are you uncomfortable taking time out to do nothing at all? What thoughts come to mind when you consider doing nothing? I've heard countless women tell me that "doing nothing equals laziness" and, operating under such a deception, these dear ones could not slow down, let alone *stop,* without tremendous guilt. And sitting still in guilt is no rest at all.

Take another look at our scripture for today. Concentrate on the gentle sweetness of Jesus' words: *Learn the unforced rhythms of grace...keep company with me...live freely and lightly.* Do you hear any shame in those phrases? Certainly not. This passage reflects the heart of God toward us—loving tender, inviting. He will not *force* us to join Him in rest. He simply calls to our hearts, drawing us closer and allowing us the opportunity, and ultimately, the *choice*, to come.

Will you dare to cast down the accusatory thoughts that would have you believe rest and guilt go hand-in-hand? God is calling to you today to slow down, exhale your anxiety, and get away with Him. Trust Him, take Him up on His invitation, and He will show you how.

FOOD FOR THOUGHT

1. What comes to mind when you think of the word *rest*?

2. If you find you have difficulty slowing down, what do you suppose tends to get in the way? How will you challenge those obstacles today?

3. Re-read Matthew 11:28-30 (read it in several translations if you have them). Which part of Jesus' invitation speaks to you most? Why?

4. Challenge yourself to designate a time for resting in the Lord today. If you can't see how to fit it into your schedule, ask God to clear your calendar and trust that He will. After your time of rest (even fifteen minutes is a good start), use your journal to record your experience. What was difficult for you? What thoughts, judgments, or distractions came up for you? If the experience was refreshing, write out a prayer of gratitude.

Father, thank You for inviting me to rest. Help me to lay down my deceptions and distractions as I begin to prioritize my times of rest with You. I believe You will meet me in times of silence and stillness. Help me to redefine rest in my life.

Hope For The Hollow

DAY 28: CAREFUL NOW...

Don't be so naive and self-confident.
You're not exempt. You could fall flat on
your face as easily as anyone else. Forget
about self-confidence; it's useless. Cultivate
God-confidence.

1 Corinthians 10:12 MSG

One of the most troubling things I hear from women as they leave treatment is, "Oh, I'm not worried about relapse. I'm feeling really secure in my recovery." Whoa, slow down there, Recovery Rock Star! Let's get real. Recovery is hard work and relapse is often a harsh reality.

Most women don't *want* relapse to be their reality (although some actually plan it that way), but many find themselves caught off guard by a moment of weakness and lose their footing on that very slippery slope. And often, overconfidence—*self-confidence*—is what leads to their fall.

Scripture tells us that "pride goes before a fall" (Proverbs 16:18) and when we become overly confident in ourselves, we lose sight of our total need for and dependence on God, leading us into prideful thinking which is always a setup for failure.

Remember our earlier devotion about the importance of humility? When we remain humble, God Himself lifts us to new heights in recovery and in life. She who humbles herself will be exalted, and she who exalts herself will be humbled. And usually, it isn't pretty.

If you've come to a place where you feel like you've got this recovery thing in the bag, be careful. You've likely lost sight of your dependence upon the Lord. And sister, that kind of useless self-confidence is the last thing in the world you need.

Be careful not to fall back into that old, familiar trap of comparison. Just as you once used to compare yourself to others in terms of body size or "perfection," you may find yourself tempted to play the comparison game with others in recovery as well—i.e., "Well, sure, I didn't follow my meal plan exactly, but *she* never follows *hers* at all." Or, "Okay, so I skipped my therapy appointment this week. But I know a lot of women who don't even *have* a therapist." Be careful, girl; your recovery isn't about her, whoever she is. It's about you, and it's between you and God. You are partners in this, remember. That means He *won't* do it without you and you *can't* do it without Him. Or had you forgotten?

Self-confidence is useless. God-confidence will keep you focused, secure, and precisely positioned to be protected, directed, and blessed.

FOOD FOR THOUGHT

1. How do you know when you have begun to lose sight of your total need for God in recovery?

2. When have you found yourself tempted to play the comparison game, both in your disease and in recovery?

3. When it comes to your recovery, God *won't* do it without you, and you *can't* do it without Him. Do you agree? When have you tried to do it on your own? What happened?

4. Use your journal to ask the Lord for help in your recovery today. Challenge yourself to do something you have been afraid or hesitant to do; something for which you will need to rely upon God in a special way (try a "fear food" or a specific clothing challenge, for example). If you cannot think of anything, ask the Lord to bring a challenge before you. He will, and He will meet you in it, because He desires for you to grow confident in Him.

God, I admit it—I need You, as much as ever. Any progress I have made, I owe to You. You are the reason I am able to do anything at all. Apart from You, I can do nothing. I trust You today to show me new ways to rely upon You, wholly and completely.

DAY 29: BUT FOR THE GRACE OF GOD

Unless the Lord had given me help, I would have dwelt in the silence of death.

Psalm 94:17 NIV

Ever have one of those moments when suddenly you come face-to-face with the reality of your frailty as a human being? The Bible tells us that our lives are as fleeting as a vanishing vapor or mist (James 4:14), here one minute and gone the next. But many of us who struggle with addictive disorders tend to buy the lie that we are untouchable. The lives of other people may be in danger because of *their* eating disorders, but *we* are just *fine*. It's almost as if we think to ourselves, "I've got this."

I had my own reality check seven years ago when I learned of the death of my friend Cindy at the age of twenty-nine. Cindy died of sudden cardiac arrest, as a result of damage caused by her eating disorder. My first reaction to the news of her passing was anger. It just wasn't fair. But as God took me through the grieving process and the anger gave way to sadness, I began to dwell on one pervasive, overwhelming thought: *She never thought this would happen.*

That reality haunted me for years, and I have since shared Cindy's story with other women, careful not to reduce her beautiful life to a mere cautionary tale. Cindy did not intend to die from bulimia. Many had warned her about the dangers of her ED behaviors—myself included—and she had consistently responded, "I'm fine." We, of course, did not believe her, but the problem was that *she* believed herself. There was no convincing her otherwise, and now it's too late.

Attention, sisters in recovery: If you are reading this book right now, God has spared you. You are still here, and it is not by chance or by luck of the draw. God has a plan and a purpose for your life, and in His mercy, He has kept a hand of protection upon you to this very day.

Reminder: If you have an eating disorder, you have been playing with fire. If not for the grace of God, you might not have this opportunity to devote yourself and your energy to recovery. The fact that you woke up today means you have been extended another measure of mercy and grace. Another day, another chance. Make no mistake; God is doing His part in the fight for your life. Give thanks to Him today as you team with Him and do your part. You are here *and you have hope,* because of His amazing grace!

FOOD FOR THOUGHT

1. Do you believe our human lives are as fleeting as a vapor, here today and gone tomorrow? How does meditating on that reality affect you?

2. Is Psalm 94:17 true for you? What is it like to acknowledge that the Lord has "given you help" which has sustained your life?

3. Many of us with addictive disorders tend to buy the lie that we are untouchable. Does this describe you? How so?

4. If God's hand of protection upon you has given you this day as a gift, what will you do with this day to communicate your gratitude?

Father God, I humble myself before You today as I acknowledge my total dependence upon You for life. Without You to sustain me and protect me, at times from my own hands, I simply don't know where I would be today. Thank You for extending mercy to me and giving me another day and another opportunity to trust You in my recovery process. Help me to remember today that my life is Your gift to me, and what I do with it is my gift to You.

DAY 30: A NEW SONG

I waited and waited and waited for GOD. At last he looked; finally he listened. He lifted me out of the ditch, pulled me from deep mud. He stood me up on a solid rock to make sure I wouldn't slip. He taught me how to sing the latest God-song, a praise-song to our God. More and more people are seeing this: they enter the mystery, abandoning themselves to GOD.

Psalm 40:1-3 MSG

There comes a time in our recovery journey when we are overtaken by a moment—usually when we have managed to slow down and quiet ourselves before God—when we find, almost without knowing how it happened, that we are at peace. There is a stillness in our soul we have never known. If this moment has not yet occurred for you, take heart and know that yours will come.

If life is a series of peaks and valleys, we might consider the worst of our eating disorder days to be the valleys and those glorious days of sober enthusiasm for life to be the peaks. But this moment I am referring to doesn't necessarily hit you when you are in the middle of a mountaintop experience. In fact, I find it usually happens when you are just doing something mundane like driving home from work or having lunch with a friend or emptying the dishwasher, and you suddenly think to yourself, "Hey, I'm peaceful. Right now, in this moment, God is holding me. How cool is that?"

This is what it's like. You realize, often out of the blue, that God has stood you upon a solid rock, that He has lifted you out of the ditch and pulled you from the deep mud of the disease and disorder that once was such a stronghold and held you so tightly in its grasp. This is how freedom makes itself known to you. Often, it's an overwhelming feeling of gratitude in an underwhelming setting, like your kitchen table or your car, and you find that you just have to praise God for what He has been doing for you and in you.

And just as our scripture passage says, people will see and notice as they watch you living your life. Something is different about you. It's more than the restored glow of health and wellness that accompanies recovery; it's the undeniably attractive fragrance of a changed heart. People will see it and realize they are hungry for what you have. It is for this reason they, too, will want to "enter the mystery, abandoning themselves to God."

Remember, friend, your life isn't about you. Your life is about and for the glory of your creator. When He is most glorified in you, you will be most satisfied in Him. Recovery is not a climactic arrival; it is the process of growing more and more dependent upon God, and less and less dependent upon a disease. And after a while, you find your life has become a new song of praise, when you didn't even realize you'd been singing.

FOOD FOR THOUGHT

1. Have you ever been overtaken by moments of peace in your recovery? When?

2. Have you imagined that recovery would be a mountaintop experience or a climactic arrival? What have been your expectations?

3. In your own words, what might it mean to "enter the mystery and abandon yourself to God"?

4. In your journal, write out your own praise song to our God. What do you have to praise Him for today, in this very moment? This month? This year?

God is good. He is making a beautiful song—a new song—out of your life. And I, for one, cannot wait to hear it.

Father God, thank You for what You are doing in my life, and for the new song You are teaching me to sing. May others see You in and through me, and may I resemble You more each and every day, as I draw nearer to Your heart. Thank You for all that You have spoken to me through this devotional journey. Help me to apply it to my life.

WHO AM I IN CHRIST?

I AM ACCEPTED...

- I am God's child. (John 1:12)

- As a disciple, I am a friend of Jesus Christ. (John 15:15)

- I have been justified. (Romans 5:1)

- I am united with the Lord, and I am one with Him in spirit. (1 Corinthians 6:17)

- I have been bought with a price and I belong to God. (1 Corinthians 6:19-20)

- I am a member of Christ's body. (1 Corinthians 12:27)

- I have been chosen by God and adopted as His child. (Ephesians 1:3-8)

- I have been redeemed and forgiven of all my sins. (Colossians 1:13-14)

- I am complete in Christ. (Colossians 2:9-10)

- I have direct access to the throne of grace through Jesus Christ. (Hebrews 4:14-16)

I AM SECURE...

- I am free from condemnation. (Romans 8:1-2)

- I am assured that God works for my good in all circumstances. (Romans 8:28)

- I am free from any condemnation brought against me and I cannot be separated from the love of God. (Romans 8:31-39)

- I have been established, anointed, and sealed by God. (2 Corinthians 1:21-22)

- I am hidden with Christ in God. (Colossians 3:1-4)

- I am confident that God will complete the good work He started in me. (Philippians 1:6)

- I am a citizen of heaven. (Philippians 3:20)

- I have not been given a spirit of fear but of power, love and a sound mind. (2 Timothy 1:7)

- I am born of God and the evil one cannot touch me. (1 John 5:18)

I AM SIGNIFICANT...

- I am a branch of Jesus Christ, the true vine, and a channel of His life. (1 John 15:5)

- I have been chosen and appointed to bear fruit. (John 15:16)

- I am God's temple. (1 Corinthians 3:16)

- I am a minister of reconciliation for God. (2 Corinthians 5:17-21)

- I am seated with Jesus Christ in the heavenly realm. (Ephesians 2:6)

- I am God's workmanship. (Ephesians 2:10)

- I may approach God with freedom and confidence. (Ephesians 3:12)

- I can do all things through Christ, who strengthens me. (Philippians 4:13)

TWELVE STEPS OF RECOVERY

- Step 1: We admitted we were powerless over our eating disorder and that our lives had become unmanageable.

- Step 2: We came to believe that a Power greater than ourselves could restore us to sanity.

- Step 3: We made a decision to turn our will and our lives over to the care of God as we understood God.

- Step 4: We made a searching and fearless moral inventory of ourselves.

- Step 5: We admitted to God, to ourselves, and to another human being, the exact nature of our wrongs.

- Step 6: We were entirely ready to have God remove all these defects of character.

- Step 7: We humbly asked God to remove our shortcomings.

- Step 8: We made a list of all persons we had harmed and became willing to make amends to them all.

- Step 9: We made direct amends to such people wherever possible, except when to do so would injure them or others.

- Step 10: We continued to take personal inventory and when we were wrong, promptly admitted it.

- Step 11: We sought through prayer and meditation,

to improve our conscious contact with God as we understood Him, praying only for knowledge of God's will for us and the power to carry that out.

• Step 12: Having had a spiritual awakening as the result of these steps, we tried to carry this message to other people with eating disorders, and to practice these principles in all our affairs.

This version of the 12 Steps is an adaptation from the original 12 Steps of Alcoholics Anonymous.

Acknowledgements

Special thanks to Diana Flegal for being not only a top-notch agent, but a trusted friend. Thanks to the staff of Timberline Knolls, especially Dr. Kim Dennis, Tom Dattalo, and Melissa Rocchi, for their ongoing support and encouragement. Thanks to Jan Pyrce and James Gresham for seeing my potential and challenging me to live up to it. Huge thanks to Jody Mitchell, without whom I wouldn't have learned most of the wisdom contained in these pages. Thanks to Pastor Clem & Anne Walchshauser and my Three Rivers Church family. Thanks to Mom, Jaden, Bonnie, Kris, and Erica for letting me be me, for better or for worse, and for putting up with me every time I have a deadline. And above all else, thanks to my Lord Jesus, for He alone is my hope.